Developing The Royal Gift Of Tongues

Developing The Royal Gift Of Tongues

PAUL FENWICK

Byker City Fellowship International Publishers

Copyright © Paul Fenwick 2021

A CIP catalogue record for this title is available from the British Library.

ISBN

978-1-9997038-5-1

Contents

Forward

This booklet is not for those who are undecided in their minds on whether Tongues is for today or not. This booklet is for those who have already been baptised in the Holy Spirit and Fire and are speaking in Tongues. Our Father who is in heaven wants you to <u>know</u> and <u>experience</u> more of this amazing kingdom gift. The reason why I use the term Royal Gift is because a President cannot give a royal gift and a Prime Minister cannot give a royal gift, only a <u>King</u> can give a 'Royal Gift'. Tongues is a love gift given to us by our King and His Kingdom, we must view it as such.

Personal Testimony

I was born-again on the 10th August 1995 (Saturday night) in the east end of my city which is Newcastle-upon-Tyne. On Sunday the 11th the person who led me into the new birth experience (Rev. Dr. Robert Ward) asked me, "Do you want to be baptised in the Holy Spirit?" Having no church background or history I answered the question with a question, "What's that?" He told me that until I had been converted, I had been full of the demonic power of Satan, now it was time to be full of the power of God. My immediate answer was, "Yes". Then he asked me, "Do you want to speak in tongues?" Once again I answered the question with a question, "What are tongues?" Tongues I was told is a gift from God, it is a supernatural language which God gives you by and through the Holy Spirit, it enables you to talk to Him without the devil or his demons being able to understand what you are saying. This explanation might not have been your experience but for me and the life I had just been set free from it was extremely relevant and important, my answer again was, "Yes!"

On 11th August 1985 at 7.30pm I attended my first evening meeting in a small community centre in the east end of the city. A visiting evangelist was there that night and after he spoke it was announced that it was time for prayer and the laying of hands. When my turn came for prayer the evangelist asked me, "Do you want to be baptised in the Holy Spirit?" My answer was "Yes." He told me to close my eyes and he laid his hands upon my head. What happened next is hard to explain in words, but it seemed like I was immediately and intensely electrocuted with fire. It didn't happen gradually nor did it come in waves or surges. It was instant, intense and constant, both internally and externally I was in the grip of this electric fiery experience.

Then from deep within something started to bubble, then the bubbling sensation grew and grew until it erupted into my chest and then exploded out of my mouth in a loud clear language I had not learned.

"I had been baptised in the Holy Spirit and Fire, and I was speaking in tongues."

At the end of the evening the evangelist told me to pray in tongues every day for fifteen minutes, this would keep my soul and body connected to the electrifying power and fire God had put in my spirit; this was very wise counsel considering what was to come.

I no longer pray in tongues for fifteen minutes each day, the Royal Gift of Tongues is now a lifestyle (1 Corinthians 14:18). I believe that the baptism of the Holy Spirit and fire, with speaking in tongues is absolutely essential for the times in which we live.

The devil does not respect theology, doctrine or religion, he only understands power and authority and that is what the baptism of the Holy Spirit and Fire gives the believer.

The Royal Gift of Tongues is a God given gift that opens the way for the Fire, Power and Glory to flow from the spirit of the believer into the world (Mathew 3:11-12; Luke 24:49; John 7:38-39; Acts 1:8; Acts 2:2-4; Acts 10:44-48; Acts 19:1-7; 1 Corinthians 14:2, 4a,18; Rev 1:15b, 16b).

Tongues is a Royal Gift of Grace given by our King Jesus who is in heaven, to His Kings, Priests and Ambassadors (2 Corinthians 5:20; 1 Corinthians 14:18) who are here on earth, so that His invisible kingdom which is in Heaven, will be manifest on this visible earth, causing His Kingdom to forcefully advance and to be established.

The defination of an Ambassador is: A diplomat of the highest rank and a skilled negotiator sent to another country as a permanent respresentative from his or her own nation. An Ambassador's only purpose in life is to represent the Government or Kingdom which called and appointed them.
Diplomatic immunity is the right of every Ambassador
(Isaiah 54:17).

I believe that as you meditate (Joshua 1:8) on the statements made in this booklet and put them into REGULAR PRACTICE (James 2:17), your soul life and physical life will change and you will rise up and into into:

- New levels of God.
- New levels of Intimacy with the Holy Spirit.
- New levels of Power and Dominion in your daily life.

- Higher levels of Divine Health.
- Higher levels of Power towards the enemy.
- Higher levels of Love towards mankind.
- Higher levels of Self-Control towards yourself.

- Increased Spiritual Momentum and Growth.
- Increased Capacity to carry the Holy Spirit.
- Increased Awareness of the Moving and Direction of the Holy Spirit.

Paul Fenwick
Byker City Fellowship International

Introduction

In the latter part of the 20th century and now in the 21st century the abiliy to be <u>diligent</u> seems to be a disappearing quality.

A good defination of the word <u>diligent</u> is:
To be determined and focused until the end result is achieved.

This is not an attitude nurtured in today's instant, credit card, buy now pay later society. The word of God says, **"Jesus set His face like flint."** A <u>diligent</u> person does not give in, or stop half way. As Kingdom representatives here on earth we must set an example, by faith in the power of the Holy Spirit on how to live a life individually and corporately in the area of diligence. We must be a people who allow God to finish what He started in us, no matter what the cost. The <u>diligent</u> application of the Royal Gift of Tongues enables the Breakthrough Believer to achieve the desired end result.

Proverbs 12:24 – **"The hand (power and ability) of the diligent will rule (have dominion)."**

Tongues is a Royal Gift of Grace given to us by our King Jesus so that we, His annointed kings and priests, can by faith release heaven into earth and kingdom order into the demonic chaos that is at work on the earth and in our cities. Our cities do not belong to the devil, they belong to our King Jesus.

Psalm 24:1 – **"The earth is the Lord's, and everything in it, the world, and all who live in it."**

He has given us delegated authority to go into the world, and in His Name (Position, Authority and Character), advance His Kingdom.

Psalm 45:1 – **"My tongue is the pen of a skilful writer."**

Isaiah 50:4 – **"The Sovereign Lord has given me an instructed tongue to know the word that sustains."**

After my conversion, (10th August 1985) the Holy Spirit gave me the scripture Isaiah 50:10b, **"Who walks in darkness and has no light? Let him trust in the name (position, honour and character) of the Lord, and rely upon his God, (El-o-heem)."** This scripture has been an anchor to my soul in times of darkness. During those times, praying in English was ineffective and unproductive, but praying in tongues has been the breakthrough gift that has lifted my soul above the storms and repositioned me in the light.

There has been times when the Holy Spirit has released the interpretation of the tongues being prayed. Three examples of these poetic interpretations have been included in this booklet.

Being able to pray in tongues is truly a life saving, soul restoring and mind renewing gift.

The Royal Gift of Tongues is:

- A Key that opens the way for Divinely Inspired Thought and the Prophetic Word of God.
- Not restricted by time or space.
- The God given vocal connection between the invisible realm of the spirit and the visible realm of man. The Holy Spirit is the inter-realm connector; He connects the two realms together, the invisible and the visible. As we, God's annointed kings and priests in the order of Melchizedek, stand by faith, praying in the spirit no matter what the circumstances, what is in the realm of the invisible will be made manifest by the Holy Spirit and the ministering angels.

His Kingdom will come and his will, will be done.
Only believe.

The Royal Gift of Tongues enables the kings and priest of God to self encourage and motivate. This keeps them in a high level of Hope, Faith and Inspiration, enabling them to encourage and motivate those around them to move forward and keep moving forward. The inner spiritual strength released by praying in tongues is crucial and essential for the 21st century believer and the times we are living in. The devil knows that his time is short therefore we, as God's representatives here on earth, must be daily in the place of power, love and of a sound mind (2 Tim 1:7) in order to frustrate the plans of the enemy (2 Corinthians 2:11 – **"For we are not unaware of the devils schemes."**) and advance the Kingdom of God.

The Royal Gift of Tongues enables the kings and priests of God to pick up the spiritual strings of the Holy Spirit and move on with strong conviction towards their God given destiny and also to successfully shift gear into whatever the Holy Spirit is doing at any given time or place. Our King Jesus likens the Holy Spirit to a wind in John 3:8 and a river in John 7:38-39. The Royal Gift of Tongues keeps us flexible and fluid as we move in time with the Holy Spirit, keeping a loose hold on our own plans and programmes; this gives us the ability to change direction at any time as the Holy Spirit directs. Our ability to move with the Holy Spirit as He moves is essential for the advancement of God's Kingdom here on earth and in this world.

1. Give Me Your Word

Lord, give me your Word and illuminate my mind
Lord, give me your Word so your truth I can find
Lord, give me your Word that is my hearts burning desire
Lord, give me your Word and send your Holy Fire

Lord, give me your Word that will break the chains
Lord, give me your Word that will release the latter rains
Lord, give me your Word that is my hearts desire
Lord, give me your Word and send your Holy Fire

Lord, give me your Word that will open the eyes of the blind
Lord, give me your Word the treasures of darkness to find
Lord, give me your Word that is my hearts burning desire
Lord, give me your Word and send your Holy Fire

Lord, give me your Word that will heal the damage and distress
Lord, give me your Word so that others I can bless
Lord, give me your Word that is my hearts burning desire
Lord, give me your Word and send your Holy Fire

Lord, give me your Word and reveal the power of your Blood
Lord, give me your Word and cause me to walk in that which is
good
Lord, give me your Word that is my hearts burning desire
Lord, give me your Word and send your Holy Fire

Lord, give me your Word the powers of darkness to tear down
Lord, give me your Word to walk the world wearing the Victors
Crown
Lord, give me your Word that is my hearts burning desire
Lord, give me your Word and send your Holy Fire

2. The Royal Gift Of Tongues

The Calling, Ministry, Anointing(s) and Destiny of the believer are in the Spirit. Operating in tongues on a daily basis will bring about birth, growth and maturity in all four of these areas.

The Word of God tells us very clearly that:

- We were crucified with Christ (The Anointed King) Romans 6:6.
- We died with Christ (The Anointed King) Romans 6:8.
- We were buried with Christ (The Anointed King) Romans 6:4.
- We were raised with Christ (The Anointed King) Ephesians 2:6.
- We have been seated with Christ (The Anointed King) Ephesians 2:6, in the highest heavenly realm.

So as we exercise our Royal Gift of Tongues, we do so from a position of Faith, Victory and Dominion. Hebrews 11:1 tells us that **"Faith is the substance of things hoped for."** Our hopes must be founded and grounded in the things of God; this allows the Spirit of Faith and the angels to go to work as we pray in tongues.

The Royal Gift of Tongues is a vocal faith gift and there will be times when the individual sons and daughters of God do not feel like praying in tongues due to negative circumstances (internal or external). These negative feelings or circumstances must be strongly resisted and as we do this by **Faith** we will get the **Victory** (Romans 9:33b). The victory will position us in a place of **Dominion** and then we can declare with confidence:

1 John 4:17 – **"As He is, so am I in this world."**

Genesis 1:26 – **"For I am made in his image and likeness and he has given me dominion."**

Isaiah 54:17a – **"Therefore no weapon formed against me can prosper!"**

Psalm 23:1 – **"Because the Lord is my shepherd I want for nothing."**

Proverbs 10:20 – **"The tongue of righteous is as choice silver."**

Tongues is not a something, tongues is Someone.

Testimony

At the end of one of our Sunday night meetings, at about 10pm as the Holy Spirit had us praying corporately in tongues for a considerable time, I was approached by one of the people in attendance, who gave me this testimony. He had arrived at the start of the meeting at about 6.30pm. He had just checked his mobile phone for messages and having noticed that the battery was low he turned his mobile phone off and placed it in the inside pocket of his jacket. At the end of the meeting he decided to check his mobile again and was very surprised to see that the battery on his mobile phone was fully charged.

Our King is interested in every detail of our lives no matter how small. Praying by faith in strong corporate tongues releases resurrection life (James 5:6b), and the recharging of the mobile phones was a sign to us that everything else we had been praying for – and more – had been done. (Isn't God amazing).

Ephesians 3:20 Amp – **"Now to Him who, by (in conseuence of) the [action of his] power that is at work within us, is able to [carry out His purpose and] do superabundantly, far over and above all that we [dare] ask or think [infinitely beyond our highest prayers, desires, thoughts, hopes or dreams]."**

Personal Testimony

While attending a prayer meeting with about one hundred christian students on the 31st October (Halloween) the specific purpose of which was to stand against the spirit of witchcraft*[1] and its activities in our city (Newcastle-Upon-Tyne, England) and its activities in the churches of our city. There came a time when we

1. See appendix A- Religious Witchcraft

were led by the Holy Spirit to pray corporately in strong focused tongues.

At the end of the meeting at about 1am, a student (whose nationality was Swedish) came over and thanked me for bringing much needed direction to her life. She said he had been wrestling with a very important decision for about ten days but on that night he had received the answer.

She told me that she had heard me say very loudly and very distincly in Swedish (a language I do not speak) 'don't do it – don't do it – don't do it.' She left that prayer meeting after having an encounter with God and knowing very clearly what she must do and what she must not do.

The Royal Gift of Tongues is one of the ways that our King Jesus by the Holy Spirit brings direction to His sons and daughters here on earth, frustrating the plans of the enemy and keeping us on the Highway of Holiness (Isaiah 35:8-10). So that we can walk in our God given purpose and fulfil our kingdom destiny.

Proverbs 16:1- **"The answer of the tongue is from the Lord."**

Focused tongues prevent you from making mistakes and wrong decisions.

Testimony by Linda Fenwick

For a number of years I have been given the privilege of going to the Philippines (Matthew 28:19-20). The lord appeared in a dream to one of the Filipino ladies and said, "When this lady comes to your nation you must get her to pray for you." We had never met before, but as I preached in her church she recognised me from the dream.

Unbeknown to me at the end of the meeting she was amongst many others who came forward for prayer. I prayed in tongues and laid my hands on this particular woman, then my spirit gave me the words to speak, I commanded her womb to open and for a child to come forth (still unaware of her situation). The following year when visiting the Philippines again the same lady came and introduced herself to me and her new baby. She had been trying to concieve for sixteen years and she took her dream by faith, and as I prayed in tongues the word of God was birthed, produced and fulfilled that woman's desire.

Proverbs 31:26 – **"The wife of noble character opens her mouth with wisdom and on her tongue is the word of kindness."**

Tongues:

1. Is the voice of the Lord (Psalm 29:3-9) carrying the Word of the Lord.
2. Is a Spirit Language that needs to be developed.
3. Is the <u>Now</u> Word of God:

- Coming out of the Presence of God.
- Released by the Spirit of God.
- Through the sons and daughters of God.
- In order to manifest the Kingdom of God.

4. Come from the Holiest of Holies and functions in three heavens.
   5. Activate the Gifts of the Spirit.
   6. Produces Great Boldness

- The word of God tells us that we are the righteousness of God in Christ Jesus (2 Corinthians 5:21) and this righteousness is through the blood of Jesus (Romans 5:9).
- In Proverbs 28:1 it says, **"The righteous are as bold as a lion."**, in the new covenant that boldness is in the spirit.
- The Royal Gift of Tongues enables the sons and daughters of God to draw upon this Holy Boldness and release it whenever it is needed.
- We cannot extend God's Kingdom with our own natural courage and understanding, only the boldness and wisdom of

the Holy Spirit will cause us to breakthrough the obstacles and every illegal hindrance the enemy sends our way.

7. Releases overcoming power and ability, positioning us so that we can receive the Hidden Manna (Revelation 2:17).

8. Edifies (embolden, construct and build up) the believer (1 Corinthians 14:4).

9. Release and bring about the manifestations of the blessing in Ephesians 1:3 – **"We have been blessed with every spiritual blessing in the heavenly realms in Christ."**

- The invidual son and daughter of God must be able to access these spiritual blessings while ministering here on earth.
- The Royal Gift of Tongues is a Kingdom Key given by God so that we his kings and priests can open the doors of our spirit here on earth and see His Kingdom come and His Will be done.
- The Holy Spirit is the administrator of Gods Kingdom here on earth.
- The Royal Gift of Tongues enables the Breakthrough Believer to see things from a heavenly perspective and by faith keep the unlimited resources of heaven accessible.

Proverbs 10:22 Amp – **"The blessing of the Lord – it makes [truly] rich, and he adds no sorow with it [neither does toiling increase it.]"**

10. Cleanse and build correct Godly atmosphere's internally (soul) and externally (our world) (1 Corinthians 14:2, :4; 1 Corinthians 2:14-16).

11. Bring about expansion, development and increased capacity for the things of God in the soul of the believer, enabling them to function and flow more efficiently in the things of God (1 Corinthians 14:4).

12. Releases angels, which are ministering spirits (Hebrews 1:14), sent from heaven to minister to the heirs of Salvation (In the Greek: So-tay-ree-ah) *Meaning: deliverance, health and safety.*

Angels only respond to the Will and Word of God, they are constantly listening for the voice of His Word (Psalm 103:21-22).

When praying in tongues the Will and Word of our Lord God and King Jesus is being released through His kings and priests here on earth. This allows the angels to move and carry out the Will and Word of God. It is very important that as we are praying in tongues individually and corporately we do not stop until the angels have finished their assigned task. The Holy Spirit will give you an inner witness when the job is done. As God's kings and priests stand by faith praying in tongues, the angels are enabled to advance the Kingdom of God here on earth.

13. Bring answers from God and Revelation of Great and Unsearchable Things all of which in our spirit because we have the mind of Christ.

Isaiah 50:4 – **"The Sovereign Lord has given me an instructed tongue to know the word that sustains the weary."** Jeremiah 33:3 – **"Call to me and I will answer you and tell you great and unsearchable things you do not know."**

14. Bring:

- Revelation
- Repentance
- Refreshing
- Revealing
- Restoration
- Reformation
- Removal
- Revival

(Acts 3:18-26)

15. Need to be focused, whatever you are praying about in tongues, keep your mind locked onto the end result. The end result is what God's word says about their situation.

Praying in the spirit identifies obstacles that hinder the progress of the believer. When praying in tongues, the Holy Spirit will release understanding so that these obstacles can be removed, making the way smooth and straight, so that the individual son and daughter of God can walk in their purpose (original intent) and advance the Kingdom of God.

As the sons and daughters of God pray in tongues by faith, this will cause them to walk in the opposite spirit to the world (Kosmos). This will dislodge internal demonic influences. It will starve and deaden wrong attitudes and ungodly thought patterns, thereby keeping the believer on the pathways of righteousness and the Highway of Holiness.

Verse 20 of Jude says – **"Build yourself up in your most holy faith, praying in the Holy Spirit."**

The flesh and the forces of darkness are continually trying to resist and stop the believer from speaking, praying or singing for long extended periods of time. If the believer resists the flesh and the devil and presses in with the Holy Spirit in tongues, the flesh will be brought into subjection and the powers of darkness will suffer defeat. The soul of the believer will be victorious and become dominant in their world. Jesus does not want us out of the world (John 17:15-18), but to be salt and light in the world, a lamp on a stand and a city on a hill which cannot be hidden.

Personal Testimony

I was once asked if I would speak at an evening meeting at a Baptist Church. The subject I was given was, 'The Joy of the Lord is Your Strength', Nehemiah 8:10. I asked the Holy Spirit how should I prepare for this meeting (this particular church was not known for it's high levels of Joy). The strategy I received was to pray in tongues for <u>six hours</u> on the day of the meeting, which I did (Isaiah 1:19). After arriving at the church, and the singing and announcements were finished, I took the microphone and read Nehemiah 8:10. Not more than twenty minutes into the message, the whole congregation (about one hundred people) erupted into laughter, shouting and other manifestations of joy, and by the end of the night the whole church were dancing the Conga! Being obedient to the Holy Spirit, released the Power of the Spirit and brought the Kingdom of Heaven into that church! (Matthew 6:10; Romans 14:17).

Psalm 51:14 **"My tongue will sing of your righteousness."**

Psalm 71:24 **"My tongue will tell of your righteous acts all day long."**

This is the place where heaven and earth connect and merge (Matthew 6:10). Kingdom Power, Divine Health and Abundant Life all break out from within us, through us, and upon us, and like King David, we can say:

Psalm 16:11 **"For you have shown me the path of life, and in your presence is the fulness of joy, and at your right hand are eternal pleasures for evermore."**

Psalm 23:1 **"For you O Lord, are my shepherd, guide and protector, and I want for nothing."**

Psalm 62:7 **"For in you is my salvation and my glory."**

Psalm 84:10 **"For better is one day in your courts than a thousand elsewhere."**

Throughout the 20th Century and now in the 21st century, every nation involved in a war or major conflict has used and is using secret code (this was also true during the cold war). These codes are used to keep sensitive information out of the hands of the opposing forces.

If the enemy does not know what you are going to do, he cannot intercept or stop you. Every man-made code can be broken, no matter how complicated or high tech they are, but in our conflict (Ephesians 6:2) our King has given His Ambassadors their own personal vocal code (tongues) that the enemies of our King cannot break or intercept. When speaking in tongues, by faith, the enemies of the Kingdom of God are unable to understand what we are saying. So let us **"Pray in the spirit on all occasions,"** keeping the devil ignorant and the forces of darkness confused.

When Operating In The Royal Gift of Tongues:

1. Gods Perfect Will is being spoken out of your spirit and is being released into the situation that is being prayed about (1 John 5:14-15).
2. You are never at fault in what you say (James 3:2).
3. You are speaking the <u>Truth</u> and there is no slander coming from you (Psalm 15:2-3).
4. Words of Divine Life are flowing out from within the believer (Proverbs 18:21).
5. You are taking up the Shield of Faith (Praying in tongues is done by faith).
6. You are using the sword of the Spirit (Tongues is the rhema Word of God).
7. Allow the Holy Spirit to bring expression and emphasis to your words.
8. Allow the strength of your spirit to flow through your voice in tongues.
9. Don't allow your mind to drift, keep it focused.

The body of the believer is the Temple of the Holy Spirit, so allow Him to develop prophetic actions to accompany our spirits flow, as you pray and sing in tongues.

- Rivers of living water are flowing from the believer (John 7:38-39).
- This causes God's Word (seed) to germinate, grow and mature in the life of the believer (Luke 8:11).
- This keeps them in step with the Holy Spirit and opens up new pathways and opportunies for the Kingdom advancement.

Every son and daughter of God, when speaking in tongues, is releasing the language of life and words of life (Proverbs 18:21).

Focused Tongues:

1. Is not something you do, tongues is a lifestyle.
2. James 3:6 says, **"The tongue is a fire, a world of iniquity.",** verse 8 says, **"no man can tame the tongue it is an unruly evil full of deadly poison."** When we pray in the spirit we are allowing the Holy Spirit to take control of our tongues thereby changing the source of our words from the soul to the spirit. Jesus says in Matthew 15:18-19 – **"Those things that proceed out of the mouth come from the heart (soul) and they defile a man for out of the heart (soul) proceed evil thoughts, murders, adulteries, fornication, theft, false witness and blasphemies."** So if we never want to be at fault in what we say (James 3:2b), we must allow the Holy Spirit to control our tongues, praying in the spirit releases a constant flow of divine kingdom life which keeps us on the highway of holiness.
3. Is like the eagle launching itself off the edge of its nest: Tongues takes you higher in the spirit like the soaring eagle.
4. Keep you:

- On the <u>WAY.</u>
- In the <u>TRUTH.</u>
- Always full of <u>LIFE</u> (Greek:Zoe) Tongues is the language of life and Jesus has sent the Holy Spirit so that you may have abundant life.

5. Builds up the walls (Nehemiah 4). This is done by faith because faith is your shield, protection and defence.

6. Builds you up, prepares you and removes the internal and external obstacles out of the way, so that the Kingdom can advance and become established in and through you (Isaiah 57:14 **"Build up, build up and prepare the road! Remove the obstacles out of the way of my people"**).

7. Cause the sword of the Lord to be used and released by the Holy Spirit through you (Revelation 1:16).

8. Enlarge the place of your tent (Isaiah 54:2), increasing your capacity.

9. Practiced for long regular periods, cause your Soul and Body to become tuned into the Presence of God.

10. Allow you to hear the Presence of God, the presence of God is not a something but a someone.

Shared Testimony

While attending a bible study on the 20th May 2008, which was being led by my very good friend Pastor Tom Leighton, the Holy Spirit took me into a trance like state and I started to re-live and re-experience my baptism in the Holy Spirit. (Read my testimony in the Forward of this booklet).

After this experience, Jesus spoke very clearly into my mind these words, 'Give Tom what I gave you!' After a short time Pastor Tom Leighton handed the meeting over to me, I then explained to everyone present (about twelve people in total) what had happened and what the Lord had told me to do, I then asked everyone to stand, close their eyes and pray in tongues. While everyone was praying in tongues, I became aware that I should walk down the centre of the room away from Pastor Tom and then turn and face him, all the while praying in strong tongues. This I did, and when I turned I had a mental picture of walking towards him and taking hold of his hands. I was also aware that I must continue to pray in the Spirit, and so I approached him praying in loud tongues and took hold of his hands, the next part of this testimony is in Pastor Tom Leightons own words:

'I was teaching from Jeremiah 1:4-10. The atmosphere was thick with the presence of God so much so that the Holy Spirit was manifesting in those in the room. After I finished speaking, Pastor Paul Fenwick stood up and asked everyone to stand with him, close their eyes and begin speaking in tongues, which they did.

I was aware that Paul was approaching me; I was standing with my head bowed and my hands clasped in front of me. I opened my eyes and looked forward over the top of my spectacles. Paul had changed into fire, and nothing was visible. Two hands came forward out of the fire and took hold of my hands, these hands were not Paul's hands, they were the hands of Jesus. How do I know that they were the hands of Jesus? I saw the marks where the nails had been.

Jesus held my hands and there was a surge of Power going through me which I can only describe as electricity. I could not pull my hands from his, it was if they were fused together. His fire was burning yet there was no heat only the terrific Power surge going through me. I could not stand still I was jumping and moving from side to side, my whole body felt weightless.

My hands have not been the same since that moment. The palms of my hands continue to be smooth and shining as though they had been oiled. I know that the Lord is preparing me for a new season and taking me to a new level'.

I believe that as we allow the Holy Spirit to develop and mature the Royal Gift of Tongues; 'That which eye has not seen, we will see, that which ear has not heard, we will hear and that which has not entered into the mind of man we will know by revelation and experience'.

The pre-pared things have been revealed to us by the Holy Spirit in our spirits and as we pray in tongues these revelations move from our spirit into our understanding (1 Corinthians 2:10).

Proverbs 15:2 – **"The tongue of the wise uses knowledge correctly."**

Focused Tongues:

1. Act as a Spiritual Indicator or Radar and develops the believer's spirit in the area of Intuition as well as Power.
2. Develop a God Consciousness in your Body and Soul*[2] and makes you physically aware of the prescence of god on a daily basis. Jesus said **"Never will I leave you or forsake you."** (Hebrews 13:5). 1 Corinthians 6:19 says; **"Do you not know that your body is a temple of the Holy Spirit, who is in you, who you have received from God.** That means His presence is constantly with us twenty four hours a day, seven days a week, but sadly this is only a mental concept to so many believers and not a daily experience. Praying in tongues by faith will cause this awareness to become a daily reality producing new levels in God and an increasing depth of intimacy with Jesus.
3. Prevent you from being surprised or ambushed by the enemy's deceptive ways, works and schemes (1 Corinthians 2:11).
4. Provide you with a high level of Divine Efficiency in every area of life.
5. Matthew 28:18 says, **"Then Jesus came to them and said, all authority in heaven and on earth has been given to Me."**

Colossians 2:15 (Amp) says, **"(God) disarmed the principalities and powers that were ranged against us and made a bold display and public example of them, in triumphing over them in Him and in it (the cross)."**

Takes you through the valley of the shadow of death (Psalm 23:4).

All the devil can do is send shadows to intimidate the sons and daughters of God (Job 3:25). If the devil can get you to believe in a shadow then he has access to your thoughts, and access to your thoughts gives him power in your life. The devils illegal kingdom is

2. *Soul = mind, will and emotions.

a kingdom of shadows, but there is no substance in a shadow and shadows have no power or authority.

Our Kingdom is a Kingdom of Love (1 John 4:8), and a Kingdom of Light (1 John 1:7), a Kingdom of Fire (Hebrews 12:29), and of Power (1 Corinthians 4:20). As sons and daughters of God, we have been given the spirit of faith which is the, **"Substance of things hoped for."**

<u>"We belong to a kingdom of substance not shadows"</u>

6.Releases:

- God's creative power into the situation you are focusing in on.
- Your internal Anointing which is in your spirit, into your external atmosphere which is your soul body and the world you inhabit.
- Takes you into a place of Revelation and the Presence of God.
- The Royal Gift of Tongues causes songs of deliverance to rise from within your inner man and surrounds you with the Presence of God (Psalm 32:7).

7. Take you out of anxiety of the soul* [3] and puts you into the place of Spiritual Peace and Rest (Isaiah 28:11-12).

8. Stir up the Gifts and fans into the Flame the Spirit within you. It is the nature of fire to spread, increase and consume.

9. Keep the believer constantly connected to the Spirit of Grace and Divine Favour; this is essential for victory and success.

- Praying in tongues will enable you to receive fresh revelation and insight about the Royal Gift of Tongues.
- Praying and singing in tongues will release the internal River of Fire and Life which is in your spirit.
- Praying and singing in tongues gives you access to and activates the Heavenly Wells of <u>Salvation</u> (In the Hebrew: Yesh-oo-ah) (Isaiah 12:3).

3. soul= mind, will and emotions

The defination of Salvation is: Deliverance, Aid, Victory,
Prosperity, Health and Welfare.

Jesus says that the Kingdom of God is within (Luke 17:21b) and it is written in 2 Peter 1:3, that we have been given all things that pertain to life and godliness according to His divine power. The Royal Gift of Tongues is a Kingdom Key that opens the door and allows the invisible Kingdom of the Spirit into the visible realm of the earth.

Thy Kingdom (invisible) come, thy will (invisible) be done, here on earth (visible) as it is being done in Heaven (invisible).

"The Two Shall Become One"

Tongues is the Will and Word of our King being released from the third heaven into the first and second heavens. When His Will is declared and the Word of the King of Kings goes out, no matter what the situation it has to bow its knee, change and come into line with His <u>Kingdom</u> Governmental will. God the father did not send Jesus to planet earth to start a new religion. Religion has never been the fathers plan. God's original plan for man is written in Genesis 1:26-30. The Father bestowed upon Jesus a government. Isaiah 9:6c says, **"And the government shall be upon His shoulders."**, and then in verse seven we are told what type of governemnt this will be, **"Of the <u>increase</u> of His government and <u>peace</u> there will be <u>no end.</u>"**

The defintions of:
Kingdom: A domain or realm ruled over by a King.
Increase: To enlarge, multiply, excel and to grow abundantly.
Peace: Health, prosperity, favour, rest, safety.
No End: Eternal and forever.

Every son and daughter of God is here on earth to represent the King of Kings and His heavenly government. This Heavenly Kingdom Government has been increasing on planet earth for over two thousand years; nobody has been able to stop it and nobody will. The Holy Spirit is the administrator of this government and He does this through the sons and daughters of God, there is no religion or earthly government that can stop the increase of the government of our King here on earth.

The Royal Gift of Tongues has nothing to do with religion, tradition or denominations. Tongues is a language which has been freely given to us by our Father so that we His Ambassadors can freely communicate with Jesus our King:

- Every Ambassdor of every government here on earth has a direct line to their President or Prime Minister.
- Every Ambassador on assignment must have the technology to communicate with their President or Prime Minister.

The Royal Gift of Tongues is our direct line to Jesus our King, day or night the line is always open.

Praying in strong focused tongues for extended periods of time will empower and enable the dependent believer to become a Breakthrough Believer; this causes soulish dependence to fall away and liberates the sons and daughters of God.

A breakthrough Believer is a son or daughter of God who has come into the realisation that they have the God given internal ability to stand-up on their own spiritual feet in any situation and forcefully extend and advance God's Kingdom here on earth, whenever or wherever the Holy Spirit directs. Breakthrough Believers and the Governmental Churches they belong to have the ability to move in the NOW anointing of God, producing results that will fulfil the purposes (original intent) of God in their city or whichever city God sends them to. They allow this to happen supernaturally and the Holy Spirit works through them. The Royal Gift of Tongues is a vocal sign of that in-dwelling anointing. The devil hates the anointing and God's anointed because that was who he was, and that was what he lost (Ezekiel 28:14).

As the sons and daughters of God stand by faith and pray in tongues, the total defeat and humiliation by Jesus our King over the devil is being vocally declared in three worlds. Every time the Breakthrough Believer speaks in tongues, it is a vocal sign that we have been given back the Dominion that was lost in the Garden of Eden. Jesus did not come to earth to restore a religion, Adam did not hand a religion over to the devil in the Garden. Jesus came to earth to restore back to Man what was lost in the Garden of Eden, Relationship, Fellowship, Dominion.

The defination of a Breakthough is:
To achieve success after a prolonged and lengthy effort.
A significant advance that removes barriers to progress.
The act of removing, surpassing or overcoming an obstruction or obstructions (Psalm 18:29).
A militant advance through and beyond an ememy's defences.
A significant development or discovery.

Psalm 39:3b – **"As I meditated the fire burned, then I spoke with my tongue."**

The Pioneer Spirit within a Breakthrough Believer, is fanned into flame through the Royal Gift of Tongues. Every fire needs oxygen and fuel, meditating on the 'now' (rhema) word of God and praying in the Spirit will keep the fire of the Holy Spirit burning brightly within you (snakes dont like fire).

The defination of a Pioneer is:
An explorer of new lands and regions.
An originator or developer of something new.

As the sons and daughters of God stand by faith praying in tongues the Holy Spirit will make known to them and position them to receive:

- The Riches of His Glory, Romans 9:23.
- The Riches of His Grace, Ephesians 1:7.
- The Unsearchable Riches of Christ, Ephesians 3:8.
- His Riches in Glory, Philippians 4:19.

The defination of Riches is: wealth, money, possessions, abundance and valuable bestowments.

There is no shortage, lack or recession in heaven and the command of our King Jesus is that we are to ask our Father who is in heaven, to cause His Kingdom and His will to manifest in every area of our lives here on earth.

As sons and daughters (2 Corinthians 6:16), kings and priests (Rev 1:6) and citizens of the Kingdom dwelling in the household of God (Eph 2:19), by faith the Royal God given Gift of Tongues enables the Holy Spirit and the ministering angels to position us or re-position us so that we can receive, partake of and release the Riches of our King and His Kingdom into the world that we inhabit.

Good communication releases resources

Operating in Holy Spirit led tongues for extended periods of time produces:

1. A deepening of the relationship between soul and mind of the believer and the Spirit of Jesus. Every relationship depends on good communication; good communication will cause continuous growth, depth and development in relationships. The Royal Gift of Tongues is the heavenly language that our Father who is in heaven has given us so that we can

communicate with Him and Jesus our King on a spiritual level, so that our mind, emotions and understanding which are in the soul will not get in the way, contaminate or influence what we are saying. The more time we spend talking to someone the more we get to know them.

2. Unity by the Holy Spirit, thereby releasing the Anointing and Blessing of God which are in the spirit, this enables the people of God to throw off the lies of the enemy and move out into the streets, businesses, homes and schools of their cities and extend the Kingdom of God, because the most important people in our cities are those that are not yet born again.

The Royal gift of Tongues is a personal love language given to the bride by the bridegroom, so that she can pour out her heart to Him from a place of deep burning passion and fervent intimacy.

I believe that the Song of Songs is one of the most inspirational, energising and life giving books in the Word of God.

In Song of Songs 4:6 it says; **"Until the day breaks and the shadows flee away, I will go to the mountain of myrrh and the hill of frankincense."**

Song of Songs 5: 5 and 5:13 speak of:

- Hands and fingers dripping with myrrh (to unlock and release).
- Lips dripping with Myrrh (to speak the word of life). (Psalm 45:2b; Luke 7:6; John 6:68)

This is a picture of the place of Anointing and being Anointed.

Myrrh has been used in the Middle East for many centuries; it was used to get rid of constipation, intestinal worms, kill mosquitoes and other human parasites. This is the place of internal cleansing and external protection (2 Tim 2:20-21).

Psalm 45:8 says, **"All your garments are scented with myrrh."** As kings and priests of God here on earth we have been given this anointing.

The Royal Gift of Tongues is a God given key, which opens the spiritual door allowing the anointing oil of myrrh to flow into an demonic activity operating internally or externally. The Royal Gift of Tongues also releases the spiritual fragances of God into the situation (2 Corinthians 2:14-16).

Isaiah 10:27 says, **"The yoke will be destroyed because of the anointing."** Praying in tongues is one of God's Kingdom Keys for releasing that yoke destroying anointing into the areas of enemy activity.

"The anointing is for action!"

3. The Living Word

The Living Word is a sword in my hand
The Living Word reveals to me the fathers plan
The Living Word illuminates my way
The Living Word is like the Sun at noonday

The Living word is a burning fire in my soul
The Living Word strengthens me and makes me whole
The Living Word gives me Faith and Power for today
The Living Word guides me along life's highway

The Living Word brought by the Holy Ghost
The Living Word releases the angelic host
The Living Word renews the spirit of my mind
The Living Word reveals hidden treasures that are mine to find

The Living Word brought me out of darkness into light
The Living Word that causes me to win every fight
The Living Word which keeps me on the path of righteousness
The Living Word my guide along Gods highway of holiness

The Living Word my shield in times of war
The Living Word a key which opens every door
The Living Word the Rock on which I stand
The Living Word keeps me firmly and forever in my Fathers
loving hand

4. The Royal Gift of Tongues Is A Spiritual Weapon

Tongues and Spiritual Warfare

1. Tongues causes the Hammer (the word) of God to be applied in hard situations (Jeremiah 23:29b).
2. Tongues releases the Power of God towards and into any area of demonic oppression or control, causing a breakthough release and freedom. (Isaiah 30:27 –**"And His tongue is a consuming fire."**)
3. Tongues release the Life of Jesus from the spirit into the soul and body of the believer and demolishes and flushes out familiar spirits*[1] and strongholds of death, which have been built up in the soul of the believer.
4. Strong Holy Spirit led tongues enables you to become the Strong Man of your atmosphere.

The Royal Gift of Tongues is a Holy Consuming Fire in the mouth of God's kings and priests. As they stand by faith and pray in tongues, the consuming, devouring Fire of God will expose and drive out the enemy in any and every situation (snakes dont like fire) (Isaiah 30:27; Jeremiah 5:14; Acts 28:3-5).

Personal Temstimony

1. See Appendix B - Familiar Spirits

Whilst participating in a joint denominationl youth meeting at a Baptist Church, I was asked to lead the prayer team (eight people and myself). Whilst the service was on we prayed in strong tongues and declared the word of God as the Holy Spirit led us. About forty five mintues into the meeting one of the prayer team received what she believed was a Word of Knowledge about a young woman who was heavily into witchcraft and was at the youth meeting downstairs (the room we were using was above the main auditorium where the meeting was being held). I accepted this word and focused our prayers accordingly.

Later one of the leaders of the minsitry team came up and asked me if I would come downstairs and pray with a young woman who was heavily into witchcraft, I said "Yes," knowing inwardly that was going to be easy, the job had already beeen done. I asked the young lady if it was alright for me to pray for her, and I was about to rebuke the spirit in the name of Jesus, but no sooner had I laid my hands upon her head she screamed, jack-knifed in her chair and was totally released from the spirit of witchcraft. Her eyes were bright and her face was glowing; she left that meeting free and totally transformed. This all came about because of obedience to a divinely inspired thought while praying in tongues (See Introduction of this booklet).

Psalm 119:171a – **"My lips overflow with praise."**
Psalm 119:172a – **"My tongue will sing of your word."**

Tongues and Corporate Spiritual Warfare

Strong corporate Holy Spirit led tongues:

1. Enables God's legal representatives (the Governmental Church) to become the Strong Man over their Holy Spirit designated area.
2. Dislodge and cast down illegal Governmental powers.
3. Raises the spiritual water level in their city / area and this will

cause the declaration and demonstration of the Kingdom of God to increase publicily.

4. Levels the mountains and raises up the valleys. Breaks down the bronze gates and cuts through iron bars. Releases the treasures of darkness and the riches stored in the secret places. This is because the Ambassadors of God are united in representing the Kingdom of God in the cities into which God has sent them.

The plans for our cities were settled in God's heart before the creation of planet earth and the solar system it inhabits. Strong corporate Holy Spirit led tongues release Divine Strategies from the Holy Spirit for your city.

Jeremiah 29:7a and 7c say:

"Seek (ask) the peace (shalom) of the city."

"Pray to the Lord for it, for in its peace (shalom) you will have peace (shalom)."

The defination of Shalom is: safety, welfare, health, prosperity, favour and rest.

God's word never changes (Psalm 119:89). What He commanded the Isrealites to do in Babylon through Jeremiah, He has commanded us to do through the Holy Spirit. Pray for the safety, welfare, health, prosperity, favour and rest of our cities.

Shalom

Personal Testimony

In the word of God there is an account of Jesus forgiving and healing a paralysed man (Luke 5:17-26).

The Holy Spirit gave me this passage as a strategy for my city. He said that the city of Newcastle-Upon-Tyne was like the paralysed man, he could not get to Jesus himself, and our city did not have the ability to get to Jesus on its' own. The paralysed man needed others to carry him into the forgiving grace and healing power of Jesus and our city needs the sons and daughters of God to carry it into the presence of Jesus.

After we as a spiritual family accepted this, the Holy Spirit revealed the next part of the strategy. He said, 'Pray for the health of the city', and then He broke that down into eight specific components:

1. Pray for the Spiritual Health of the city.
2. Pray for the Mental and Emotional Health of the city.
3. Pray for the Physical Health of the city.
4. Pray for the Political Health of the city.
5. Pray for the Financial Health of the city.
6. Pray for the Educational Health of the city.
7. Pray for the Marital Health of the city.
8. Pray for the Parental Health of the city.

We have, and we are faithfully putting this strategy into operation and we are seeing significant results. '*A strategy is the correct approach in achieving the desired, targeted purpose, by using all of the resources and talents available.*' (Isaiah 51:16; 55:11; James 5:16b). Because we are not only praying, but we are boldy declaring and demonstrating the Kingddom of God on the streets of our city.

"He that believes in Me as the scripture says, (Proverbs 18:4; Isaiah 12:3; 44:3; John 4:14)**, out of his belly shall flow rivers of living water** (John 7:38) **and everything will live wherever the river goes."** (Ezekiel 47:9).

Psalm 126:2 - **"Our mouths are filled with laughter and our tongues with songs of joy."**

The Royal Gift of Tongues releases the internal anointing of Joy and the Spirit of Praise, and as the Holy Spirit takes us through the gates of praise (Isaiah 60:18) we are surrounded by the walls of Salvation (deliverance, aid, victory, prosperity, health and well being). As we stand in that place by faith, the Spirit of worship will rise within us, and as we sing in the Spirit and abide in the realm of worship, then the Glory of God our Father, the Glory of Jesus our King and the Glory of His Kingdom will come upon us.

Personal Testimony

On the night of the 19th August 2013, I had an heavenly encounter with John G Lake. I was taken by the Holy Spirit to a location which seemed to be deep in enemy territory. We were surrounded by Warrior Angels, who were there to protect us. I was aware that I was sitting in a room, opposite me was John G Lake, and this is what he said:

"The key that continually opened the door to the miraculous in my life was praying in Tongues."

Then instantly I was awake and back at home. This might be hard to accept for some, but let us not limit the Holy Spirit with our own understanding, because 1 Corinthians 2:7, and Ephesians 3:20, are as real today as they were when first written.

5. Tongues - Healing and Deliverance

Tongues and Healing / Deliverance

Strong individual tongues bring about Physical Healing and Deliverance for the believer. No sickness, disease, infirmity or affliction is stronger than the Holy Spirit. As we pray in tongues and keep our minds fixed on the finished work of Christ and what His blood has done for us, then our Father who is in heaven, will give life to our mortal bodies through and by His Holy Spirit who lives in us.

Rom 8:11 – **"And if the Spirit of him who raised Jesus from the dead is living in you, He who raised Christ from the dead is living in you, He who raised Christ from the dead will also give life to your mortal bodies through his Spirit, who lives in you."**

Strong, corporate tongues brings about physical healing and deliverance for the body of Christ (The Anointed King) and the cities they are part of, because when the body of Christ (The Anointed King) set aside their differences, unite and become of one mind and one voice on behalf of their cities, God commands the blessing. The good news of the Kingdom is declared and demonstrated, strongholds of the enemy are demolished, captives are set free. Abundant life starts to flow from the Spirit into the natural and from the invisible into the visible and our cities are revived.

Psalm 51:14 – **"My tongue will sing of your righteousness."**
Psalm 71:24 – **"My tongue will tell of your righteous acts all day long."**
Proverbs 18:21 – **"The tongue has the power of life and death."**
Proverbs 12:18 – **"The tongue of the wise brings healing."**

Our bodies are the temple of the Holy Spirit and the house of

His glory. As sons and daughters of God we are here on earth as representatives of Jesus our King, and the Kingdom of heaven. Therefore our physical health, condition and appearance is extremely important as a witness to those who are not yet in the kingdom. The Royal Gift of Tongues releases resurrection life, this revitalises the body and produces greater levels of divine health and life (Job 33:25; Psalm 92:10; 12-14; Isaiah 40:29-31; John 10:10b), so we can complete and fulfil our God given destiny here on earth.

'Tongues is our God given self-repair system.'

Proverbs 15:4 – **"A wholesome tongue is a tree of life."** (Psalm 103:20-22).

Ephesians 3:20 Amp – **"Now to him who, by (insconsequence of) the [action of His] power that is at work in us, is able to [carry out His purpose and] do super-abundantly, far over and above all that we [dare] ask or think [infinitely beyond our highest prayers, desires, thoughts, hopes and dreams]."**

The Royal Gift of Tongues is a manifestation of the inner working of God's Power, doing that which only God's Power can do!

In summary I would like to draw your attention and imagination to the tremendous price that was paid by our King Jesus, so that we could receive and experience the Kingdom Power and Dominion that comes with and through the Royal Gift of Tongues (Isaiah 53:1-12). From the Garden of Gethsemane to the Cross, a journey He took on our behalf, so that we could be reconnected to the Father, and receive again the Holy Spirit.

Everything written in this booklet has been paid for in and by the Blood of our King. So read it, meditate upon it, do it and watch His Kingdom forcefully advance and His Government increase in your life and in your world.

6. Oh the Blood of Jesus

Oh the Blood of Jesus speaks to me today
Yes the Blood of Jesus guides me through the day
Oh the precious Blood has cleansed me from within
Hallelujah! The blood of Jesus has set me free from the power of
sin

Oh the Blood of Jesus is a fountain deep and wide
Yes, the Blood of Jesus brings the angels to my side
Oh the precious Blood protects me along the way
Hallelujah! The Blood of Jesus avails for me today

Oh the Blood of Jesus gives me acces to the Throne of Grace
Yes, the Blood of Jesus causes me to dwell in that secret place
Oh the precious Blood, poured out in heaven for me
Hallelujah! The Blood of Jesus has gloriously set me free

Oh the Blood of Jesus brings heaven here to Earth
Yes, the Blood of Jesus, the life of the new birth
Oh the precious Blood applied by the Holy Spirit
Hallelujah! The Blood of Jesus, it's Power knows no limit

Oh the Blood of Jesus shed on the Cross for me
Yes, the Blood of Jesus shed on Calvary's Tree
Oh the Blood of the Lamb, poured out on the Mercy Seat above
Hallelujah! For the Blood of Jesus, the Fathers perfect gift of Love

Appendix A - Religious Witchcraft

Luke 10:19

"I have given you authority to trample on snakes and scorpions and to overcome all the power of the enemy."

Ephesians 6:12

"For our struggle is not against flesh and blood, but against the rulers, against the authorities, against the powers of this dark world and against the spiritual forces of evil in the heavenly realms."

2 Cor 10:3-5

"For though we live in the world, we do not wage war as the world does. The weapons we fight with are not the weapons of the world. On the contrary, they have divine power to demolish strongholds. We demolish arguements and every pretensions that sets its self up against the knowledge of God, and we take captive every thought to make it obedient to Christ."

The purpose of religious witchcraft is:

1. Attack and destroy the Apostolic and Prophetic voice in the church.
2. To infiltrate, contaminate, seduce and then take control.

The spirit of religious witchcraft targets the minds and emotions of God's Leaders in order to hinder or de-rail the advancement of God's Kingdom in and through them. Breakthrough Leaders and Breakthrough Believers and the Governmental Chuch they are part of have the ability to break the hold of the spirit of religious witchcraft. This is because they have or are overcoming this particular stronghold and influence in their own lives and atmosphere. This particular spirit targets Breakthrough Leaders and

Governmental Churches because they pose a direct threat to the illegal, demonic influence the devil has in, on and through the church.

The spirit of religious witchcraft will always try to exalt itself through human effort. Two of its main counterfeit manifestations in the church are prophecy and teaching. The spirit of religious witchcraft wants to be elevated to a position of power, influence and recognition in the church, so over a period of time it will draw people around itself leading and seducing them into deception and sin.

The spirit of religious witchcraft has to be attacked, overcome and removed.

It's strategy against a Leader is:

1. Deceive, seduce, control and discredit (To make powerless).
2. Intimidate, discourage, cause loss of vision, confusion, disorientation and withdrawal.
3. Depression, despair, hopelessness and defeat.

As soon as a Breakthrough Leader is aware of any of these signs, he or she must rise up into:

Breakthrough tongues

Breakthrough praise

Breakthrough proclamations

They must stay there until they get the **Breakthrough and Victory.**

Psalm 91:13; Psalm 149:6-9; 1 Tim 6:12; James 5:16c; Jude :20).

The spirit of religious witchcraft hates God's anointed leadership; it's target is the mind, will and emotions of the emerging Breakthrough Leader. If its strategy of intimidation does not work it will change its attack to praise and seduction. This snake and everything connected to it must be crushed beneath the feet of the church (Joshua 10:24-26; Luke 10:19) and driven out by the Fire of God (Isaiah 47:14, Acts 28:1-6, Revelation 18:8), so that the Spirit of Holiness can come and fill the temple.

Matthew 6:10 **"Thy Kingdom come, Thy will be done here on earth as it is in heaven, give us this day our daily <u>bread</u>."**

The <u>bread</u> of the children is deliverance from all demonic activity.

Matthew 15:22-28.

<u>Job 12:22</u>

"He reveals the deep things of darkness and brings deep shadows into the light."

<u>Dan 2:22</u>

"He reveals the deep and hidden things; He knows what lies in darkness and light dwells with him."

<u>Heb 4:13</u>

"Nothing in all creation is hidden from God's sight. Everything is uncovered and laid bare before the eyes of Him to whom we must give account."

Meditating on the scriptures below will reveal the pattern and workings of the spirit:

Judges 16:1-22; 2 Samuel 11:2-5; 1 Kings 11:1-13; 1 Kings 16:29-33; 1 Kings 19:1-4; 2 Kings 11:1-3; 13-21; Isaiah 47:1-15; Matth 14:1-12; Acts 16:16-24; Galatians 3:1; Revelation 2:18-29; Revelaion 18:1-24

Appendix B - Familiar Spirits

A familar spirit is a spirit who knows a person or place intimately. This type of spirit has become intimately accustomed and interwoven over a period of time into the lifesytle, moods and behaviour patterns of the person it inhabits. This makes them impossible to detect <u>unless</u> the Holy Spirit exposes them. When familiar spirits are in operation, the individual believes they are exercising their own free-will. In reality they are being deceived and manipulated, they are blind to the enemies activities within and through their lives. A familiar spirit works in, through and around a persons character (soul and mind). A familiar spirit knows the strengths and weakness that are in a person, and they exploit them in order to bring about the plan and strategy they have for that persons life here on earth (John 10:10).

The devil comes to steal, kill and destroy.

Familiar spirits influence and manipulate emotions and seek to control thought patterns. They know how a person will react in any given situation, they know a persons comfort zones and their explosive zones. Familiar spirits are residential spirits; they stay with an individual, a family or a specific place (haunting). Familiar spirits are generational, they become uncomfortable and agitated when they are moved from their own particular area. Mark 5:10 **"And they begged Jesus again and again not to send them out of the area."** Familiar spirits are earthbound. Luke 11:24 **"When an evil spirit comes out of man, it goes through dry places seeking rest and does not find it. Then it says I will return to the house I left."** Familiar spirits will fight against change. Denominational religion is the home of many types of familiar spirits. Religious rituals which will not, or cannot be changed are governed by familiar (religious) spirits. Just as in the natural we take on the looks of our parents or grandparents for example; eyes, ears, shape of nose and face, colour of hair, we are also born with similar personality traits, and it is in the personality (soul and mind) where familiar spirit infiltrate and reside.

Until a person is born-again they are under the control of satan and they are full of darkness and death. It is in these types of conditions that familiar spirits exist. They do not want the person they inhabit to know the truth. John 8:32 says, **"You will know the truth and the truth will set you free."** When a person is born-again that is when they can start their own personal attack against the familiar spirits that they have and are contaminating their lives.

Luke 10:19 says, **"I have given you authority to trample on snakes and scorpions and to overcome all the power of the enemy."**

2 Timothy 22:20-21 says, **"In a large house there are articles of gold and silver, also of wood and clay, some are for noble purposes and some for ignoble. <u>If a man cleanses himself</u> from the latter he will be an instrument for noble purposes, made holy, useful to the master and prepared to do any good work."**

The Kingdom (dominion) of God must be forcefully advancing in our soul, mind and body. Where familiar spirits are exposed, they must be dealt with powerfully and permanently. Job 12:22 says, **"He reveals the deep things of darkness and brings deep shadows into the light."**

Daniel 2:22 says **"He reveals deep and hidden things; He knows what lies in darkness, and light dwells with Him."**

Hebrews 4:13, **"Nothing in all creation is hidden from Gods sight, everything is uncovered and laid bare before the eyes of Him to whom we must give an account."**

The will of our Father who is in heaven, is that His blood bought sons and daughters, live lives that are totally free. The only spirit that we are to be familiar with is the Holy Spirit. So let us rise up to the challenge and drive the enemy from every corner of our soul, mind, emotions and body, so that we can be free and in the Name of Jesus, set others free and move on from one degree of Glory to the next.

Lightning Source UK Ltd.
Milton Keynes UK
UKHW030926091121
393650UK00016B/243

9 781999 703851